STATE REVENUE STAMPS

by

Martin P Nicholson

Copyright © 2015 by Martin Nicholson

All rights reserved. No part of this publication may be reproduced, distributed, or transmitted in any form or by any means, including photocopying, recording, or other electronic or mechanical methods, without the prior written permission of the author, except in the case of brief quotations embodied in critical reviews and certain other noncommercial uses permitted by copyright law. For permission requests email the author at the address below.

Martin Nicholson
Church Stretton
Shropshire SY6 7DQ
United Kingdom

Email – newbinaries@yahoo.co.uk

Some thoughts from the author

I have been a stamp collector for over 40 years, a postal historian and a philatelist for about 15 of those years and a specialist collector of revenue stamps and documents for the last 5 years. I've been a member of some the most friendly and well-run groups you could ever imagine – the State Revenue Society and the American Philatelic Society are both examples of best practice – and I even flirted briefly with philatelic exhibiting.

Despite having served such a lengthy apprenticeship I still don't have an answer to a really basic question:
> Why are postage stamps catalogued, collected and researched with so much more energy and enthusiasm than revenue stamps?

There are many countries where there doesn't seem to be a reliable and up-to-date catalogue of revenue stamps – certainly not one accessible to a virtual monoglot such as myself. I think it comes down to what I call "critical mass". Without enough revenue stamp collectors it is hard for dealers to establish a viable business, but without dealers generating catalogues and generally raising the profile of this branch of the hobby I suspect that prospective revenue stamp collectors tend to wander off into the sunset searching for easier pickings.

Thanks to the outstanding work of members of the State Revenue Society the United States of America is an honourable exception to this problem. The recently published "State Revenue Catalog", edited by Dave Wrisley, is a masterpiece of philatelic literature.

Many collectors specialise in the revenue stamps of a single USA state or on stamps issued for one particular product or service. I prefer the topical approach where my collection is based on obtaining an example of every different tax that was levied.

This small study is intended to bring to the attention of the wider collecting public the sheer diversity of state revenue stamps issued in the USA. The categories presented within the book are based on those used in the "State Revenue Catalog".

STATE REVENUE STAMPS – A TOPICAL APPROACH

ADMISSIONS	OKLAHOMA

AGRICULTURAL INSPECTION	CALIFORNIA IDAHO NEW YORK

ALCOHOL CONTAINER REFUND	IOWA

AMMUNITION	SOUTH CAROLINA TENNESSEE

AMUSEMENT DEVICE	
	ILLINOIS KENTUCKY NORTH DAKOTA OREGON

AMUSEMENT MACHINE	ARKANSAS TEXAS

APPLE ADVERTISING	
	GEORGIA WASHINGTON

APPLE MERCHANDISING	MISSOURI
APPLES	CALIFORNIA MICHIGAN
ATTORNEY AT LAW	CALIFORNIA
BEDDING 	COLORADO CONNECTICUT DELAWARE FLORIDA GEORGIA INDIANA LOUISIANA MAINE MARYLAND NEW YORK NORTH CAROLINA OHIO OKLAHOMA PENNSYLVANIA RHODE ISLAND SOUTH CAROLINA TEXAS

| | VIRGINIA |
| | WEST VIRGINIA |

BEER	ALABAMA
	ALASKA
	ARIZONA
	ARKANSAS
	COLORADO
	DELAWARE
	GEORGIA
	IDAHO
	ILLINOIS
	INDIANA
	KANSAS
	KENTUCKY
	MAINE
	MARYLAND
	MICHIGAN
	MISSOURI
	NEBRASKA
	NEW MEXICO
	NORTH CAROLINA
	NORTH DAKOTA
	OKLAHOMA
	PENNSYLVANIA
	UTAH
	VIRGINIA
	WASHINGTON
	WEST VIRGINIA
	WISCONSIN

BEER (>3.2%) BARRELS	OHIO

BEER (>3.2%) BOTTLES	OHIO

BEER (3.2%) BARRELS	OHIO

BEER CASES AND BARRELS 	MINNESOTA

BEER EXPORTED	COLORADO DELAWARE IDAHO MISSOURI NEBRASKA WASHINGTON

BEER IMPORTED	KENTUCKY NORTH CAROLINA VIRGINIA

BEER LABELS	UTAH

BEER LIQUOR AND WINE	NEVADA

BEER LIQUOR AND WINE SEALS	ALABAMA

BEER METER STAMP	NORTH CAROLINA

BEER (3.2%) BOTTLES	OHIO

BEER AND WINE	SOUTH CAROLINA SOUTH DAKOTA

BEER BOTTLE CAPS	WEST VIRGINIA

BEER BOTTLE CAPS AND CANS	ALABAMA GEORGIA KENTUCKY MICHIGAN MISSISSIPPI PENNSYLVANIA UTAH VIRGINIA

BEER BOTTLE CAPS AND LABELS	FLORIDA

BEER BOTTLE CAPS LABELS AND CANS	KANSAS

BEER BOTTLE LABELS	KANSAS

BEER BOTTLES	MINNESOTA

BEER BOTTLES AND CANS	MARYLAND OHIO

BEER CANS	IOWA

BEER CANS AND BOTTLE CAPS	SOUTH CAROLINA

BUSINESS LICENSE METER STAMPS	SOUTH CAROLINA

BUTTER	MONTANA

CANNED DOG FOOD 	NORTH CAROLINA

CARNIVAL ELECTRICAL INSPECTION	WASHINGTON

CAULIFLOWER	OREGON

CEREAL SEED	TENNESSEE

CHAMPAGNE	DISTRICT OF COLUMBIA

CHRISTMAS TREE TAGS	MINNESOTA NEW MEXICO WASHINGTON

CIGAR VENDING MACHINE	DELAWARE

CIGARETTE AND TOBACCO VENDING	MICHIGAN

BEER MILITARY 	GEORGIA UTAH

BEER NOT OVER 4%	TEXAS

BEER OVER 4%	TEXAS

BEER PROVISIONAL BOTTLE LABELS	PENNSYLVANIA

BILL OF LADING	CALIFORNIA

BILLIARDS	TEXAS

BUSINESS LICENSE 	SOUTH CAROLINA

CIGARETTE LICENSE/VENDING	MARYLAND

CIGARETTE METER STAMPS	ARIZONA ARKANSAS CALIFORNIA COLORADO CONNECTICUT DELAWARE DISTRICT OF COLUMBIA FLORIDA GEORGIA IDAHO ILLINOIS INDIANA IOWA KANSAS LOUISIANA MAINE MASSACHUSETTS MINNESOTA MISSISSIPPI MISSOURI NEBRASKA NEVADA NEW HAMPSHIRE NEW JERSEY NEW MEXICO NEW YORK NORTH CAROLINA NORTH DAKOTA OHIO OKLAHOMA OREGON PENNSYLVANIA RHODE ISLAND SOUTH CAROLINA SOUTH DAKOTA TENNESSEE TEXAS

	UTAH
	VERMONT
	VIRGINIA
	WASHINGTON
	WEST VIRGINIA
	WISCONSIN
	WYOMING

| CIGARETTE METER STAMPS NATIVE AMERICAN | FLORIDA |

CIGARETTE METER STAMPS STATE-LOCAL	FLORIDA
	MISSOURI
	NEW YORK
	TENNESSEE
	VIRGINIA

| CIGARETTE PAPERS | INDIANA |
| | RHODE ISLAND |

CIGARETTE VENDING MACHINE	FLORIDA
	KANSAS
	PENNSYLVANIA
	RHODE ISLAND

CIGARETTES	ALABAMA
	ALASKA
	ARIZONA
	ARKANSAS
	CALIFORNIA
	COLORADO
	CONNECTICUT
	DELAWARE
	DISTRICT OF COLUMBIA
	FLORIDA
	GEORGIA

CIGARETTES NATIVE AMERICAN	FLORIDA IDAHO KANSAS MINNESOTA NEBRASKA NEVADA NEW MEXICO NEW YORK NORTH DAKOTA OKLAHOMA TEXAS WASHINGTON WISCONSIN
CIGARETTES STATE-LOCAL	MISSOURI NEW MEXICO NEW YORK OHIO VIRGINIA
CIGARETTE VENDING MACHINE 	DELAWARE IOWA NEW HAMPSHIRE NEW JERSEY WASHINGTON
CIGARS	ALABAMA ARKANSAS DELAWARE GEORGIA LOUISIANA MISSISSIPPI TENNESSEE VIRGINIA

	HAWAII
	IDAHO
	ILLINOIS
	INDIANA
	IOWA
	KANSAS
	LOUISIANA
	MAINE
	MARYLAND
	MASSACHUSETTS
	MICHIGAN
	MINNESOTA
	MISSISSIPPI
	MISSOURI
	NEBRASKA
	NEVADA
	NEW HAMPSHIRE
	NEW JERSEY
	NEW MEXICO
	NEW YORK
	NORTH CAROLINA
	NORTH DAKOTA
	OHIO
	OKLAHOMA
	OREGON
	PENNSYLVANIA
	RHODE ISLAND
	SOUTH CAROLINA
	SOUTH DAKOTA
	TENNESSEE
	TEXAS
	UTAH
	VERMONT
	VIRGINIA
	WASHINGTON
	WEST VIRGINIA
	WISCONSIN
	WYOMING

By the same author and also available from Amazon

British and Commonwealth Revenue Stamps

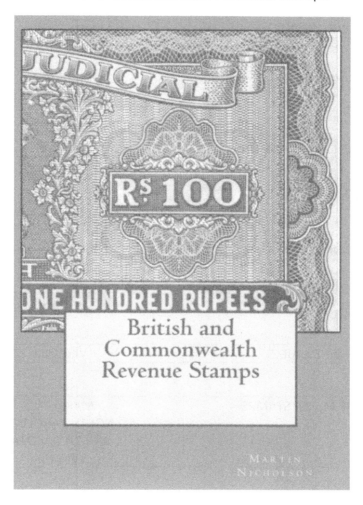

WINE CASE	INDIANA MINNESOTA

WINE DOMESTIC	ARKANSAS

WINE EXPORT	ARKANSAS

WINE EXPORTED	KENTUCKY TEXAS

WINE IDENTIFICATION	KANSAS

WINE IMPORTED	ARKANSAS

WINE IN TRANSIT	WASHINGTON

WINE KEG	INDIANA

WINE LABELS	VIRGINIA

WINE METER STAMPS	MARYLAND NORTH CAROLINA NORTH DAKOTA VIRGINIA

WINE WITHDRAWN	TEXAS

WITHDRAWN WINE	WISCONSIN

	MISSOURI
	NEBRASKA
	NEW MEXICO
	NORTH CAROLINA
	OHIO
	OKLAHOMA
	PENNSYLVANIA
	TENNESSEE
	TEXAS
	VIRGINIA
	WASHINGTON
	WEST VIRGINIA
	WISCONSIN

| WINE AND BEER | MISSISSIPPI |

| WINE AND LIQUOR | COLORADO |
| | MINNESOTA |

| WINE AND LIQUOR TAX PAID | COLORADO |

| WINE AND MIXED BEVERAGE | |
|  | OHIO |

| WINE BOTTLE CAPS AND SEALS | WASHINGTON |

WALNUTS	CALIFORNIA

WATER MELON	ARIZONA

WEIGHTS AND MEASURES	ALABAMA
	ARIZONA
	CALIFORNIA
	FLORIDA
	GEORGIA
	ILLINOIS
	IOWA
	KENTUCKY
	LOUISIANA
	MAINE
	MARYLAND
	MASSACHUSETTS
	MISSISSIPPI
	MISSOURI
	NORTH CAROLINA
	OKLAHOMA
	OREGON
	PENNSYLVANIA
	TEXAS
	VIRGINIA
	WASHINGTON

WINE	ALASKA
	ARIZONA
	DISTRICT OF COLUMBIA
	GEORGIA
	ILLINOIS
	INDIANA
	KANSAS
	KENTUCKY
	LOUISIANA
	MARYLAND
	MICHIGAN

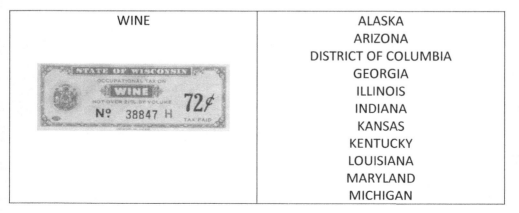

TOMATOES	CALIFORNIA VIRGINIA

TOYS	PENNSYLVANIA

TRADING STAMP	UTAH

TURKEY	VIRGINIA

TURKEY TAGS	CONNECTICUT

VEGETABLE SEED	TENNESSEE

VEGETABLE TAGS	OKLAHOMA

VENDING	WASHINGTON

VENDING CIGARETTE	ARKANSAS

VENDING DEVICE	ARKANSAS

VENDING FOOD	MINNESOTA

VENDING MACHINE	DISTRICT OF COLUMBIA MARYLAND SOUTH DAKOTA

WALL BOX	ARKANSAS

TERRAPIN TAGS	SOUTH CAROLINA

TOBACCO 	ALABAMA ARIZONA GEORGIA LOUISIANA MAINE MISSISSIPPI NEW MEXICO OKLAHOMA RHODE ISLAND SOUTH DAKOTA TENNESSEE

TOBACCO HAND-STAMPS	TENNESSEE

TOBACCO METER STAMPS	MAINE RHODE ISLAND TENNESSEE

TOBACCO PRODUCTS	NEW HAMPSHIRE

TOBACCO SEED	KENTUCKY

TOMATO AND CUCUMBER	WASHINGTON
TOMATO SEED	PENNSYLVANIA

STRAWBERRIES	ARIZONA
STRAWBERRY PLANT TAGS	ALABAMA
SUCTION DREDGE PERMIT	CALIFORNIA
SWEET POTATO	TEXAS
SWEET POTATO ADVERTISING	GEORGIA
SWEET POTATO PLANT CERTIFICATION	ALABAMA
SWEET POTATO TAGS	ALABAMA LOUISIANA MISSISSIPPI
SWEET POTATOES	CALIFORNIA NORTH CAROLINA
SYRUPS AND SOFT DRINKS	PENNSYLVANIA
TANGERINES	FLORIDA
TAX ON INVESTEMENTS	NEW YORK
TERMITES	CALIFORNIA
TERRAPIN	SOUTH CAROLINA

SOFT DRINKS	KENTUCKY LOUISIANA NORTH CAROLINA SOUTH CAROLINA WEST VIRGINIA
SOFT DRINKS BOTTLE CAPS	PENNSYLVANIA
SOFT DRINKS BOTTLE CAPS AND CANS	SOUTH CAROLINA WEST VIRGINIA
SOFT DRINKS BOTTLES AND CANS	NORTH CAROLINA
SOFT DRINKS CANS AND BOTTLE TOPS	LOUISIANA
SPORTING GOODS	ARIZONA
STAMPED PAPER	DELAWARE HAWAII MARYLAND MASSACHUSETTS NEVADA NEW YORK VIRGINIA
STOCK TRANSFER	MASSACHUSETTS MISSOURI NEW YORK PENNSYLVANIA TEXAS
STOCK TRANSFER METER STAMPS	NEW YORK

SEED TAGS	INDIANA KENTUCKY MINNESOTA NORTH CAROLINA OHIO OKLAHOMA TENNESSEE TEXAS

SELF LIQUIDATING TAX CERTIFICATES	NORTH DAKOTA

SHAD	SOUTH CAROLINA

SHAD TAGS	SOUTH CAROLINA

SHELLFISH LABELS	MAINE

SHRIMP 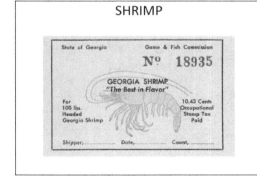	GEORGIA SOUTH CAROLINA

SHRIMP TAGS	SOUTH CAROLINA

SLOT MACHINE	MONTANA

SOFT DRINK TAGS	NORTH CAROLINA

	KANSAS
	KENTUCKY
	MAINE
	MARYLAND
	MISSOURI
	NEBRASKA
	NEVADA
	NEW JERSEY
	NEW YORK
	NORTH CAROLINA
	OHIO
	OREGON
	SOUTH DAKOTA
	TEXAS
	UTAH
	VERMONT
	VIRGINIA
	WASHINGTON
	WISCONSIN

| SEED CERTIFICATION TAGS
 | DELAWARE
IDAHO
LOUISIANA
MICHIGAN
NORTH DAKOTA |

| SEED CERTIFICATION TAGS AND LABELS | MINNESOTA |

| SEED PACKET | FLORIDA
INDIANA
NORTH CAROLINA
WEST VIRGINIA |

41

SALES	KENTUCKY

SALES TAX COUPONS	NORTH CAROLINA

SALES TAX PUNCH CARDS	OHIO

SALES TAX STAMPS	OHIO

SCALLOPS	VIRGINIA

SEAL SKINS	ALASKA

SECURED DEBT	KANSAS MICHIGAN MISSOURI NEW YORK

SEED	MINNESOTA NORTH CAROLINA OHIO TENNESSEE WEST VIRGINIA

SEED AND PLANT CERTIFICATION	MISSISSIPPI

SEED CERTIFICATION	ALABAMA ALASKA CALIFORNIA COLORADO FLORIDA GEORGIA INDIANA

PRESCRIPTION	TEXAS

PUNCHBOARD	ALABAMA
	ALASKA
	IDAHO
	MONTANA

PUNCHBOARD METER STAMPS	IDAHO

REAL ESTATE	INDIANA
	NEVADA
	NORTH CAROLINA

REAL ESTATE METER STAMPS	NEVADA
	NORTH CAROLINA

REAL ESTATE TRANSFER	ILLINOIS
	IOWA
	MISSISSIPPI
	PENNSYLVANIA
	RHODE ISLAND

REAL ESTATE TRANSFER METER STAMPS	ILLINOIS
	MICHIGAN
	NEW HAMPSHIRE
	NEW YORK
	PENNSYLVANIA
	RHODE ISLAND

RHUBARB	WASHINGTON

ROAD TAX	WEST VIRGINIA

PLANT INSPECTION	FLORIDA MAINE MISSOURI NORTH CAROLINA OREGON TEXAS WASHINGTON

PLANT INSPECTION CERTIFICATE	HAWAII

PLANT INSPECTION TAGS	KANSAS NEBRASKA

PLAYING CARDS	ALABAMA HAWAII

POLL TAX	CALIFORNIA

POTATO ADVERTISING	IDAHO

POTATO INSPECTION TAGS	HAWAII

POTATO TAGS	ARIZONA WASHINGTON

POTATOES	ARIZONA MINNESOTA VIRGINIA WASHINGTON

POWDERED MILK	GEORGIA

ORANGES	FLORIDA
OYSTER TAGS	SOUTH CAROLINA
OYSTERS	GEORGIA SOUTH CAROLINA
PACKET SEED	OHIO
PAINT VARNISH OR STAIN	NORTH CAROLINA
PASSENGER	CALIFORNIA
PEAT AND HUMUS	FLORIDA
PEAT AND HUMUS TAGS	FLORIDA
PENNY AMUSEMENT MACHINE	ARKANSAS
PESTICIDE USE	CALIFORNIA
PLANT AND NURSERY INSPECTION	CALIFORNIA LOUISIANA
PLANT AND SEED CERTIFICATES	OKLAHOMA
PLANT AND SEED CERTIFICATION	NEW HAMPSHIRE PENNSYLVANIA

37

NURSERY AND PLANT INSPECTION	INDIANA MASSACHUSETTS SOUTH DAKOTA WISCONSIN

NURSERY AND PLANT INSPECTION TAGS	MICHIGAN

NURSERY INSPECTION	MINNESOTA MISSISSIPPI VERMONT

NURSERY INSPECTION CERTIFICATES	NEW YORK

OIL	FLORIDA SOUTH CAROLINA

OIL INSPECTION	COLORADO

OLEOMARGARINE	ALABAMA GEORGIA IDAHO IOWA KANSAS KENTUCKY MINNESOTA NORTH DAKOTA SOUTH DAKOTA TENNESSEE UTAH WISCONSIN WYOMING

MORTGAGE ENDORSEMENT	NEW YORK

MOTOR FUEL LABELS AND TAGS	ILLINOIS

MOTOR VEHICLE	COLORADO IDAHO LOUISIANA MINNESOTA NORTH DAKOTA WASHINGTON WEST VIRGINIA

MOTOR VEHICLE REGISTRATION	IOWA

MOTOR VEHICLE TITLE	KANSAS MARYLAND OKLAHOMA

MUSIC BOX	MARYLAND

MUSIC DEVICE	OREGON

MUSIC MACHINE	ARKANSAS

NATIVE PLANT TAGS	ARIZONA

NURSERY AND PLANT CERTIFICATES	OHIO

NURSERY AND PLANT CERTIFICATION	GEORGIA

MALT AND WORT	INDIANA
MALT LIQUOR	ARKANSAS
MALT PRODUCTS	KANSAS
MEAT INSPECTION	CALIFORNIA
MECHANICAL GAME	ARIZONA
MELON AND TOMATO	OREGON WASHINGTON
METAL TAX METER STAMPS	SOUTH CAROLINA
MINERAL DOCUMENTARY	MISSISSIPPI
MINERAL FEED	OKLAHOMA
MIXED BEVERAGE	OHIO
MOBILE HOME	INDIANA

LIVESTOCK REMEDY 	KANSAS

LIVESTOCK REMEDY TAGS	KANSAS

LOTTERY	LOUISIANA MARYLAND

LUXURY	ARIZONA

MALT 	ARIZONA ARKANSAS IDAHO LOUISIANA MICHIGAN MISSISSIPPI OHIO SOUTH DAKOTA TENNESSEE

LIQUOR SEALS BOTTLE LABELS	ALABAMA UTAH WASHINGTON
LIQUOR SEALS FEDERAL BOTTLE STAMPS	ALABAMA IDAHO IOWA MAINE MICHIGAN MISSISSIPPI MONTANA OHIO OREGON PENNSYLVANIA TENNESSEE UTAH VERMONT VIRGINIA WASHINGTON WEST VIRGINIA WYOMING
LIQUOR SEALS PRIVATELY PRINTED	IOWA KANSAS MICHIGAN MISSISSIPPI TENNESSEE WASHINGTON WISCONSIN
LIQUOR SPECIAL	WISCONSIN
LIQUOR TAX EXEMPT	DISTRICT OF COLUMBIA ILLINOIS

LIQUOR MILITARY	GEORGIA

LIQUOR PHARMACEUTICAL	WISCONSIN

LIQUOR PHARMACIST'S	NEW YORK

LIQUOR SALES PERMIT	NORTH CAROLINA
	PENNSYLVANIA
	VIRGINIA
	WEST VIRGINIA

LIQUOR SEALS	GEORGIA
	HAWAII
	IDAHO
	IOWA
	KANSAS
	MAINE
	MICHIGAN
	MINNESOTA
	MISSISSIPPI
	MONTANA
	NEBRASKA
	NEW HAMPSHIRE
	NEW YORK
	OHIO
	OREGON
	PENNSYLVANIA
	RHODE ISLAND
	SOUTH DAKOTA
	TEXAS
	UTAH
	WASHINGTON
	WEST VIRGINIA

	WISCONSIN WYOMING

LIQUOR CASE	ILLINOIS INDIANA MINNESOTA SOUTH CAROLINA

LIQUOR CERTIFIED	INDIANA

LIQUOR EXPORTED	ARKANSAS DELAWARE FLORIDA GEORGIA KENTUCKY LOUISIANA SOUTH CAROLINA TEXAS

LIQUOR IDENTIFICATION LABELS	KANSAS TEXAS

LIQUOR IMPORTED	KENTUCKY

LIQUOR LABELS	PENNSYLVANIA

LIQUOR MEDICINAL	WEST VIRGINIA

LIQUOR METER STAMPS	MARYLAND MISSOURI NORTH DAKOTA SOUTH CAROLINA

LEVEE TAX TAGS	MISSISSIPPI

LIME TAGS	NORTH CAROLINA

LIMES	FLORIDA
	NORTH CAROLINA

LINSEED OIL	NORTH CAROLINA

LIQUOR	ALASKA
	ARIZONA
	ARKANSAS
	CALIFORNIA
	DELAWARE
	DISTRICT OF COLUMBIA
	FLORIDA
	GEORGIA
	ILLINOIS
	INDIANA
	IOWA
	KANSAS
	KENTUCKY
	LOUISIANA
	MARYLAND
	MISSOURI
	NEBRASKA
	NEW MEXICO
	NEW YORK
	NORTH DAKOTA
	OKLAHOMA
	PENNSYLVANIA
	SOUTH CAROLINA
	SOUTH DAKOTA
	TENNESSEE
	TEXAS
	VIRGINIA

KEROSENE	KANSAS MISSOURI

KEROSENE INSPECTION	NORTH CAROLINA

KEROSENE TAGS	NEBRASKA

KEYSTONE BOTTLE LABELS	PENNYSLVANIA

LAB FEE	COLORADO

LAND PLASTER	NORTH CAROLINA

LAND PLASTER TAGS	NORTH CAROLINA

LARD SUBSTITUTE	SOUTH DAKOTA

	SOUTH DAKOTA TENNESSEE TEXAS UTAH VIRGINIA WASHINGTON WEST VIRGINIA WISCONSIN WYOMING
INSECTICIDE OR FUNGICIDE	GEORGIA LOUISIANA NORTH CAROLINA
INSECTICIDE OR FUNGICIDE PARIS GREEN	LOUISIANA
INSURANCE	CALIFORNIA OREGON
INTANGIBLES	INDIANA
INTANGIBLES TAX METER STAMP	INDIANA

HONEY IMPORTED	ARIZONA

HONEY LABELS	ARIZONA

HOUSING PERMITS AND STANDARDS	WISCONSIN

ICC CAB CARD STAMPS	ALABAMA ARIZONA ARKANSAS CALIFORNIA COLORADO CONNECTICUT FLORIDA GEORGIA IDAHO ILLINOIS INDIANA IOWA KANSAS LOUISIANA MAINE MASSACHUSETTS MICHIGAN MINNESOTA MISSISSIPPI MISSOURI MONTANA NEBRASKA NEW HAMPSHIRE NEW MEXICO NEW YORK NORTH CAROLINA NORTH DAKOTA OHIO OKLAHOMA RHODE ISLAND SOUTH CAROLINA

FRUIT	GEORGIA WASHINGTON

FUR TAGS	TENNESSEE TEXAS

GAMBLING	MINNESOTA NEBRASKA NORTH DAKOTA WASHINGTON

GASOLINE	KANSAS MISSOURI NORTH CAROLINA

GASOLINE INSPECTION	ARKANSAS

GASOLINE TAGS	NEBRASKA

GRAPEFRUIT	FLORIDA

GRASSES AND CLOVERS (SEED)	TENNESSEE

HONEY 	ARIZONA ARKANSAS NEW MEXICO WASHINGTON

FERTILIZER TAGS	ALABAMA
	ARIZONA
	ARKANSAS
	FLORIDA
	GEORGIA
	ILLINOIS
	INDIANA
	KANSAS
	LOUISIANA
	MISSISSIPPI
	MISSOURI
	NEW MEXICO
	NORTH CAROLINA
	SOUTH CAROLINA
	TENNESSEE
	TEXAS
	VIRGINIA
	WEST VIRGINIA

FIREWORKS AND FIRE SAFETY	CALIFORNIA
	WASHINGTON

FLOWER BULBS	
	WASHINGTON

FOOD AND DRUGS	CALIFORNIA

	ILLINOIS
	INDIANA
	IOWA
	KANSAS
	KENTUCKY
	LOUISIANA
	MINNESOTA
	NEBRASKA
	NEW MEXICO
	NORTH CAROLINA
	NORTH DAKOTA
	OHIO
	OKLAHOMA
	SOUTH CAROLINA
	SOUTH DAKOTA
	TEXAS
	VIRGINIA
	WEST VIRGINIA

FERTILIZER	ALABAMA
	ARIZONA
	COLORADO
	FLORIDA
	GEORGIA
	ILLINOIS
	INDIANA
	KANSAS
	KENTUCKY
	MISSISSIPPI
	MISSOURI
	NEW MEXICO
	NORTH CAROLINA
	SOUTH CAROLINA
	VIRGINIA
	WEST VIRGINIA
	WYOMING

FERTILIZER LABELS	KENTUCKY

FEED 	ALABAMA ARIZONA ARKANSAS CALIFORNIA COLORADO FLORIDA GEORGIA INDIANA IOWA KANSAS KENTUCKY LOUISIANA MICHIGAN MINNESOTA MISSISSIPPI NEBRASKA NEW MEXICO NORTH CAROLINA NORTH DAKOTA OHIO SOUTH CAROLINA TENNESSEE UTAH VIRGINIA WEST VIRGINIA

FEED INSPECTION TAGS	ARKANSAS MISSISSIPPI

FEED METER STAMPS	NORTH CAROLINA SOUTH CAROLINA VIRGINIA

FEED TAGS	ARIZONA CALIFORNIA COLORADO FLORIDA

	MAINE MONTANA NEW JERSEY NEW MEXICO NORTH CAROLINA OHIO OKLAHOMA OREGON PENNSYLVANIA TEXAS VERMONT VIRGINIA WASHINGTON WYOMING
EGGS CARTON	FLORIDA
EGGS CASE	FLORIDA
EGGS CERTIFICATE OF QUALITY	CALIFORNIA INDIANA
EGGS HAND STAMPS	INDIANA
ELEVATOR	CONNECTICUT
ELECTRICAL INSPECTION	WASHINGTON
EXCHANGE	CALIFORNIA
FARM IMPLEMENT	OKLAHOMA

	NEBRASKA
	NEVADA
	NORTH CAROLINA
	NORTH DAKOTA
	OKLAHOMA
	RHODE ISLAND
	SOUTH CAROLINA
	SOUTH DAKOTA
	TENNESSEE
	TEXAS
	UTAH
	WASHINGTON
	WISCONSIN

EGG CANDLING	ILLINOIS
	IOWA
	MINNESOTA
	WISCONSIN

EGG CANDLING CERTIFICATES	MISSOURI
	SOUTH DAKOTA

EGG INSPECTION	ARKANSAS

EGG METER STAMP	ARIZONA

EGGS	ALABAMA
	ARIZONA
	COLORADO
	GEORGIA
	HAWAII
	IDAHO
	ILLINOIS
	INDIANA
	KANSAS
	KENTUCKY

	FLORIDA HAWAII LOUISIANA MAINE MARYLAND MASSACHUSETTS MINNESOTA NEBRASKA NEVADA OKLAHOMA PENNSYLVANIA SOUTH CAROLINA TEXAS VIRGINIA WASHINGTON WEST VIRGINIA

DRINKS AND SYRUPS	MISSOURI

DRIVERS LICENSE METER STAMP	GEORGIA TEXAS

DRUGS	ALABAMA ARIZONA COLORADO CONNECTICUT HAWAII IDAHO ILLINOIS IOWA KANSAS KENTUCKY LOUISIANA MAINE MASSACHUSETTS MINNESOTA

CRAB MEAT 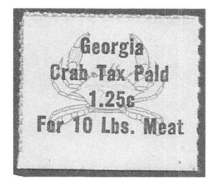	GEORGIA SOUTH CAROLINA

CRAB TAGS	SOUTH CAROLINA

DAIRY PRODUCTS	WASHINGTON

DMV INFORMATION REQUEST	CALIFORNIA

DOCUMENTARY METER STAMPS	CALIFORNIA DELAWARE FLORIDA HAWAII MAINE MARYLAND MASSACHUSETTS MINNESOTA NEBRASKA OKLAHOMA SOUTH CAROLINA WASHINGTON

DOCUMENTARY STAMPS	ALABAMA ARKANSAS CALIFORNIA

COSMETICS 	ARIZONA OHIO

COTTON	LOUISIANA

COTTON SEED MEAL	GEORGIA MISSISSIPPI

COTTON SEED MEAL INSPECTION TAGS	ARKANSAS

COTTON SEED MEAL TAGS	GEORGIA NORTH CAROLINA

COTTON SEED TAGS	MISSISSIPPI

CLEANING AND PRESSING 	NORTH CAROLINA

COIN OPERATED DEVICE	OKLAHOMA VIRGINIA

COIN OPERATED DEVICES	SOUTH CAROLINA

CONCORD GRAPES	CALIFORNIA

CIGARS AND CIGARETTES	GEORGIA
CITRUS BEVERAGE	FLORIDA
CITRUS FRUIT	FLORIDA TEXAS
CITRUS FRUIT ADVERTISING	FLORIDA
CITRUS FRUIT HAND-STAMPS	TEXAS
CITRUS FRUIT PRORATION	TEXAS
CITRUS FRUIT PRORATIONING	FLORIDA
CITRUS FRUIT QUARANTINE	TEXAS
CLAM TAGS	SOUTH CAROLINA
CLAMS	SOUTH CAROLINA

Made in the USA
Las Vegas, NV
30 September 2024